Think Like a Sniper
Trade Like a Sniper

Precision, Patience, and Mastery in the Markets

ANIL P DEV

NOTION PRESS

NOTION PRESS

India. Singapore. Malaysia.

"This book is dedicated to my family and friends who have been a part of my journey in the markets."

Thank you!

Contents

Preface

In a world flooded with flashing charts, breaking news, and endless alerts, modern traders are at war with distraction, overanalysis, and emotional noise. The markets are a battlefield - not for the impulsive, but for the disciplined. Not for the aggressive, but for the precise.

This book is not for those who believe more trades mean more profits. It is for those who are ready to step away from the chaos and step into the mind of a sniper - a master of patience, discipline, and deadly accuracy.

A sniper doesn't fire at everything that moves. He waits. He studies the terrain. He calculates. And when the time is right, he pulls the trigger with confidence, knowing everything is aligned.

The same philosophy applies to trading.

Think like a sniper: wait for the setup.

Trade like a sniper: execute with clarity.

And walk away knowing your edge wasn't luck - it was skill.

This is my second book on trading, following Timeless Market Wisdom – Winning Without Losing, which offered a comprehensive roadmap across trading psychology, strategy, risk management, and mindset development.

That book was designed to be expansive - to guide traders through the full terrain of what it takes to survive and thrive in the markets.

But this one is different.

Think Like a Sniper, Trade Like a Sniper is not about covering everything. It's about doing less - with surgical precision. This is a field manual, not an encyclopaedia. It's built for traders who are overwhelmed by noise and ready to anchor their decisions in clarity, calmness, and confidence.

This book is built around a simple yet transformative idea: trading is not a game of constant action - it's a craft of calculated decisions. The markets reward precision, not frenzy. Consistency, not chaos. And above all, emotional mastery over technical clutter.

Inside, you'll learn how to:

- Think in terms of risk before reward
- Build a target zone for high-probability trades
- Wait with discipline and strike with strategy-backed precision
- Control emotions like a sniper controls breath under pressure
- Create a trading routine that is deliberate, data-driven, and durable

This isn't another technical manual filled with indicators or market jargon. It's a book of mindset and mastery - of filtering out the noise and locking onto what matters. It's about developing the calm, confident trader within you.

Whether you're a seasoned participant or a focused learner ready to shift gears, this book is your lens, your scope, to see the markets with purpose and act with precision.

We'll move through mindset, strategy, and discipline - because all three are essential for true mastery in the markets. You'll find sniper analogies throughout, not as metaphors for entertainment, but as reflections of timeless truths: that waiting is a skill, clarity is power, and one good shot is worth a hundred random ones.

In the end, this book won't just give you tactics - it will give you a new way to see the markets, and yourself, as a trader.

Welcome to the way of the sniper.

Let's begin.

SECTION ONE

The Sniper's Mindset

1. The Art of Waiting

Why Patience Is a Trader's Most Dangerous Weapon

"It is not the most aggressive who survive in battle or in markets - it is the most patient, the most precise, the most prepared."

The markets, much like a battlefield, are filled with noise, price ticks like footsteps in the distance, volatility like crossfire, and economic data like sudden environmental shifts. Amidst this chaos, the average market participant believes that success lies in movement, in action, in being constantly present. But the true master knows differently.

The sniper-trader does not hunt by chasing. They wait. They watch. They analyse and anticipate with stillness. Their shot, much like their trade, is not frequent, it is fatal. In this lies the paradox: The less you trade, the better you trade. The more you wait, the sharper you become.

This chapter is an exploration of the art of waiting, not passive inaction, but calculated patience. A strategic stillness backed by knowledge, confidence, and control. Patience is not the absence of action; it is the presence of purposeful restraint.

The Psychology of Restraint: Mastering the Internal Battlefield

At the core of sniper-like trading lies a psychological battlefield - one not against the market, but within oneself. The undisciplined mind seeks comfort in motion. It wants to trade because it hates uncertainty, and it confuses *activity* with *progress*. But restraint demands a different wiring: it requires **emotional detachment, clarity, and high self-regulation**.

To understand restraint is to understand that every trade is not an opportunity - many are traps laid by randomness, market makers, and your own impulsiveness. Trading is a business of probabilities, not certainties. And when you accept that, the urge to act on every price move dies down.

The sniper learns to conserve energy for the perfect moment. They do not shoot to soothe boredom, or because they fear missing the kill. They shoot only when all their internal criteria are satisfied. This requires the trader to adopt a mindset shift - from the *need to trade* to the *need to wait until the edge is unmistakably present*.

Emotional capital, not just financial capital, must be preserved. Each emotional overreach weakens your psychological stamina. Restraint, then, is an act of capital conservation - the kind that makes consistency possible over the long term.

Overtrading: The Enemy of Precision

Overtrading is a symptom of psychological leakage - an invisible illness of the impatient trader. It arises from fear (of missing out), pride (need to prove oneself), or the desire to fix past losses. But like a sniper who gives away his position by firing too often, the overtrader exposes themselves to unnecessary risk, fatigue, and drawdowns.

It is important to understand that the market will always tempt you. Its primary job is not to reward you - it is to **test you.** The best trades are not just technically sound; they are psychologically clean. No urgency. No desperation. No inner conflict.

Overtrading manifests in many forms:

- Chasing entries because you fear the move has already started
- Taking marginal setups just to stay active
- Revenge trading after a loss to quickly make it back
- Trading based on opinion, not system criteria

True market mastery begins when you stop needing the market to validate your skill or your mood. When you can let the market move without feeling the need to be involved, you are trading from a place of true power.

Every great sniper knows this: You do not fire to feel in control. You fire because you are in control.

Knowing When Not to Act: The Silent Skill of Elite Traders

There is an invisible skill that distinguishes elite traders from the rest - the ability to know when *not* to engage. Most books focus on entries, exits, and setups. Few teach you the real game: *the discipline to stay out.*

In the sniper's world, some environments are too dynamic, too unpredictable to offer a clean shot. Similarly, some market phases - like consolidations, illiquid sessions, or event-driven whipsaws - offer poor trade conditions even if price seems to move.

The sniper-trader recognises that absence of clarity is a trade signal in itself - one that says: **"Stand down. Observe. Let the dust settle."**

Here's when not to act:

- When your **edge isn't present** - even if the market is moving

- When **price is moving erratically** without directional follow-through

- When you are **emotionally charged** - after a loss, argument, or personal stress

- When the trade is driven by **hope, fear, or boredom**

- When **major news events** are about to hit and invalidate technicals

This non-action is not weakness - it is **strategic detachment**, a moment of intelligence where others react emotionally. As traders, our job is not to participate in every move - it is to **survive the uncertain and strike at the inevitable.**

Building Patience into Your Trading System

Patience should not be left to chance or emotion. It must be **engineered into your trading system**. Like a sniper's checklist before a shot, your trade setup should have strict entry protocols - conditions that must all align before you are permitted to act.

This means:

- **Predefined criteria** for entry and exit (technical, fundamental, or behavioural)

- A **watchlist routine** that filters high-probability candidates

- **Timeframe discipline** (e.g., acting only on end-of-day confirmations or closing candles)

- Clear guidelines on what constitutes a **non-tradeable environment**

Your trading plan should not only tell you *what to do* - it should tell you *what not to do*. Build *gaps of inaction* into your process. This could mean only trading during specific time windows, limiting the number of trades per week, or forcing yourself to **journal every trade idea you did not take** and why.

This discipline will train your mind to find satisfaction not in trading, but in **executing the right process**, whether or not it leads to immediate profits

The Inner Evolution: From Shooter to Sharpshooter

There's a moment when a trader evolves - when the game is no longer about profit, but about precision. When your trades start to feel fewer, calmer, more refined - and your decisions no longer rely on hope or excitement, but on **data, timing, and readiness** - you are stepping into sniper mode.

This inner evolution is silent. It won't be visible in your P&L right away. But you'll feel it in your mind:

- Less stress
- Less screen addiction
- More control over your time
- Deeper trust in your edge

And above all - a quiet confidence that whispers: "I don't need the market to move right now. I'll wait. I'm prepared to do nothing until everything aligns."

This is the art of waiting. And it is, indeed, the trader's most formidable advantage.

2. Target Lock

Developing Laser-Sharp Focus in a Noisy Market

A sniper does not wake up to chase targets. He does not operate out of urgency or chaos. He operates from an unshakable stillness - a disciplined internal state of readiness, matched with precise external awareness. He may spend hours in absolute silence, observing without blinking, waiting for the perfect alignment of variables before he even contemplates action.

This is not inaction. This is **focused intent**. This is **target lock**.

In trading, as on the battlefield, this same level of intent is not optional - it is essential. The markets today are not merely fast-moving; they are cluttered with noise. Prices fluctuate constantly, headlines scream for your attention, algorithms inject volatility in milliseconds, and social media bombards your mind with conflicting narratives. Amidst this disarray, the undisciplined trader becomes reactive, scattered, and emotionally compromised.

But the sniper trader? He remains calm. He operates in slow motion even when the world around him speeds up. His focus is not on everything. It is on the **one thing that matters** - the confirmed target.

This chapter is about building that precision focus. It is about filtering distraction, narrowing your vision, refining your attention, and constructing a framework where **focus becomes your edge**. It is about achieving "target lock" - not only on charts, but in your mental state as a market participant.

Filtering Signals from Noise

"To the undisciplined, every movement is a reason to act. To the disciplined, only confirmation is a reason to engage."

Every trader begins their journey under the illusion that more information equals better performance. More indicators. More news feeds. More alerts. More opinions. But in reality, the inverse is true. **Information overload destroys clarity**. It creates decision fatigue. It invites cognitive dissonance and pushes traders into emotionally driven, fragmented action.

In contrast, the professional trader builds a mental filter. This filter separates **signal from noise** - not just on charts, but in thoughts, inputs, conversations, and reactions.

So what is *noise* in the markets?

- A random spike in price not confirmed across timeframes

- A news headline without contextual relevance to your trade

- A forum post shouting "Buy Now" without any real data

- An impulsive urge triggered by fear, greed, or FOMO

And what is a *signal*?

- A price breaking above a major resistance with volume and trend alignment

- A multi-timeframe confluence where Daily, Weekly, and Monthly point in the same direction

- An MACD crossover confirming momentum after price closes above the Super Trend

- A setup that fits your predefined system, with risk/reward clearly established

The sniper has no interest in scattered movement. He is not there to react to sound - he is there to act on **alignment**. In trading, your success is not built on reacting to movement but on recognising high-probability, low-noise environments.

This demands **clarity of process** and **emotional restraint**. It demands that you:

- Trade fewer setups

- Say 'no' more than you say 'yes'

- Trust your system more than your gut

- Define exactly what constitutes a "valid signal" - and ignore everything else

Noise is not your enemy - your reaction to it is. The real task is to master yourself, so your focus remains unshaken. In this stillness, you begin to see clearly.

Building Your Watchlist Like a Sniper Builds His Hit List

A sniper never roams aimlessly, hoping for a target to appear. He works from intelligence - meticulously gathered data, pre-planned movements, and high-value targets. His hit list is short. It is focused. It is intentional.

This is precisely how your trading watchlist must be constructed.

Most amateur traders build their watchlists like tourists packing for a long trip - everything goes in, just in case. The result? Overwhelm. Noise. Missed opportunities. Paralysis by analysis.

Instead, adopt the sniper's philosophy: your watchlist is not a scrapbook of market movers. It is a refined dossier of targets that meet your specific criteria. You are not looking for what is active - you are looking for what is aligning.

Let your hit list be governed by clear filters:

- Stocks above 200 EMA on the Daily timeframe - long-term strength

- EMA 50 above EMA 100, and EMA 100 above EMA 200 - trend structure confirmation

- Bullish candlestick on the Monthly - broader sentiment validation

- MACD crossover above signal line on Daily, Weekly, and Monthly - momentum synchrony

- Price above Super Trend (5,1) across all timeframes - trend confirmation

When your criteria are met, the stock moves from the radar to the crosshairs. You now have a live target - but even then, you do not engage without discipline. You wait for final confirmation. Only when everything aligns do you take the shot.

Over time, you are not just tracking symbols. You are building **intimate familiarity** - understanding each stock's rhythm, volatility, behaviour near key levels, and institutional patterns.

You are no longer just screening. You are *studying*. You are not just watching charts. You are *profiling targets*.

Focused Screen Time vs. Endless Monitoring

"A sniper does not win by staring longer. He wins by observing better."

One of the most damaging myths in modern trading is the glorification of screen time. Many believe that staring at charts all day is a sign of dedication. In truth, it is often a symptom of anxiety, fear, and lack of structure.

A sniper does not stare endlessly through the scope. He surveys, then retreats. He repositions, then resets. He rests his eye so that when it matters most, he sees with crystal clarity.

Your trading routine should reflect the same intentionality.

Structure your screen time like a sniper's mission:

Pre-market preparation is mission planning

Review your targets. Mark critical levels. Confirm alignment across timeframes. Enter the session with clarity - not noise.

Execution windows are precision zones

Observe when setups are nearing confirmation. Stay present only when your strategy demands it. Learn to step away when conditions are suboptimal.

Post-market is for debrief and recalibration

Review your trades. Journal your decisions. Reflect on your process. Refine your edge.

Avoid screen grazing

Mindless observation creates fatigue. Every minute in front of the screen should serve a purpose - are you confirming a setup, or just consuming movement?

Your brain, like your capital, must be preserved. Focus is a finite resource. Do not spend it frivolously. Protect it, sharpen it, and deploy it only when required.

Because in trading, as in combat, it is not the one who sees the most that wins - it is the one who sees *best*, and acts *last*.

When you train your eyes to see only what matters...

When you let go of the chaos and build a system around clarity...

When your attention becomes sharper than any tool in your arsenal...

You are no longer just in the markets.

You are locked on.

You are ready to execute.

You are trading like a sniper.

3. The Power of Preparation

Scouting, Setup, and Strategic Planning

A sniper does not arrive on the battlefield by accident. He has already been there - in his mind. Before a single shot is fired, there have been hours, even days, of reconnaissance. He knows the terrain, the wind patterns, the timing of his target's movements, and the exit route. His success lies not in how he pulls the trigger, but in the discipline, detail, and foresight behind every decision that precedes it.

In the markets, the trader who trades like a sniper approaches each day with the same level of preparation. He does not scan the open blindly. He does not hunt for opportunities in real time. He **plans his engagements** ahead of time. He **scouts** market conditions. He **sets up** his watchlist with intent. He develops **strategic trade plans**, so that when price reaches his level, his decision is already made.

Preparation is not just a habit. It is the gateway to mastery. It is the difference between professional precision and emotional guesswork. In this chapter, we explore how you, too, can build a sniper-level preparation routine - one that converts chaos into clarity, randomness into readiness, and uncertainty into structured opportunity.

Market Conditions and Pre-Trade Rituals

"You don't rise to the level of your strategy. You fall to the level of your preparation."

Each trading day is a new battlefield. And like a sniper studies the weather, terrain, and enemy movement before ever stepping into position, so too must the trader begin with a deep awareness of market conditions.

Market conditions are never static. They evolve - and your edge is only valid when it is aligned with the environment. For a trend-following strategy, ranging or volatile markets may be hostile territory. For a breakout setup, low-volume environments may yield nothing but false signals.

Begin your day like a sniper preparing for a mission:

What phase is the market in?

Is the index trending, consolidating, or reversing? What do the weekly and monthly charts say?

Where is volatility?

Are broader indices showing stability, or are there signs of increased uncertainty (gap opens, wide ranges, large wicks)?

What key events are scheduled?

Are there earnings reports, central bank meetings, or macroeconomic data releases that could affect sentiment?

What sectors are leading or lagging?

Just as a sniper understands enemy positions, a trader must know where capital is flowing and where it is retreating.

This is not passive scanning. This is **active scouting** - and it informs every decision you make that day.

Once your read on the environment is established, you move to your **pre-trade ritual** - a repeatable, disciplined routine that clears mental clutter and sharpens focus.

A sniper-inspired pre-trade ritual may include:

- Reviewing your trading plan and reminding yourself of your edge

- Visualising disciplined behaviour: patience, clarity, rule adherence

- Checking your watchlist against your criteria

- Setting alerts rather than obsessively watching price

- Taking a moment of stillness - to trade from a centred, grounded state

The unprepared trader walks into the market with hope. The prepared trader walks in with **intention**.

Creating a Tactical Watchlist

A sniper does not attempt to engage every enemy. He selects specific targets based on threat level, opportunity, and mission objectives. In trading, this means **curating a tactical watchlist** - not just a collection of names, but a dynamic shortlist of **high-quality, high-conviction setups**.

Your tactical watchlist is the operational extension of your scouting.

It answers these key questions:

- Which stocks are structurally aligned with my strategy?

- Which setups are close to triggering based on my criteria?
- Where is my best opportunity to apply capital today?

Build your tactical watchlist using defined filters:

Trend Alignment

Is the price above the 200 EMA on the Daily chart? Are EMA 50 > EMA 100 > EMA 200? This structure suggests underlying strength.

Momentum Confirmation

Is the MACD line above the Signal line on Daily, Weekly, and Monthly timeframes? Momentum should confirm direction.

Candle Behaviour

Has the Monthly candle closed bullish? This gives larger timeframe bias.

Super Trend Positioning

Is the price above Super Trend (10,3) across all timeframes? If not, remove it from your immediate scope.

Sectoral Tailwind

Is the stock part of a leading sector or theme? A lone wolf in a weak sector may lack follow-through.

As you apply these filters, the list shrinks - and this is a good thing. You are not looking for more. You are looking for clarity. You are not collecting charts. You are locking onto potential targets.

Each name that survives this process must then be annotated - with key levels, potential entry zones, stop-loss placements, and potential reward zones. This is not just a list - it is a tactical map.

By the time the market opens, you are not watching randomly. You are stalking your targets - with calm, measured awareness.

Trade Plans vs. Guesswork

"The plan is nothing. Planning is everything." – Dwight D. Eisenhower

A sniper does not fire because a target moves. He fires because the **plan has reached execution point**. He knows the distance, the angle, the wind speed, the trajectory - all before his finger touches the trigger.

Likewise, a professional trader never trades spontaneously. He does not guess. He **executes a prepared plan**, developed during calm hours, and only activated when the market delivers the conditions he anticipated.

A trade plan includes:

The Setup

What pattern or condition are you trading? Is it a pullback, breakout, or trend continuation? Does it meet your strategy's rules?

The Entry

What is the ideal entry trigger? Is it the break of a level, a candle close, a confirmation from MACD or Super Trend?

The Stop-Loss

At what level will you exit if you are wrong? Is it technically logical and consistent with your risk rules?

The Position Size

How much capital will you commit? Is it aligned with your risk per trade, based on your stop size?

The Exit

What is your profit-taking method - fixed target, trailing stop, or technical signal? Will you scale out?

This plan is written before the trade. It is not adjusted mid-trade due to emotion or impulse. It is either followed or skipped - no middle ground.

Guesswork is the enemy of mastery. The unplanned trader is always chasing - reacting, second-guessing, and falling into the psychological traps of fear and greed. The prepared trader, on the other hand, remains detached. He understands that trading is not about being right - it is about executing well-defined plans with consistency.

A good plan executed with discipline will always outperform a brilliant guess made in chaos.

Preparation transforms randomness into readiness. It creates mental space for calm, mechanical execution. It is what allows the sniper to stay composed under pressure - and the trader to stay objective in volatility.

You do not prepare because it guarantees success. You prepare because it builds structure, and structure enables clarity - and clarity is what turns a trader into a sniper.

4. One Shot

The sniper does not need a second shot.

He doesn't act twice because he never doubts once. He operates from preparation, not improvisation. From precision, not pressure. And when the conditions align - just once - he pulls the trigger with absolute intent, no hesitation, no second-guessing.

In that one shot lies the culmination of hundreds of hours of training, mapping, rehearsal, and control. His bullet is not just metal. It is a declaration of discipline.

This is the level of conviction the elite trader must aspire to.

In the market, the vast majority of traders live in the exact opposite mental state: they hesitate, they rush, they modify trades mid-flight, they doubt their own plans. And so, even when the market offers them the perfect opportunity - they either miss it or mangle it. They need multiple entries, multiple indicators, and still remain riddled with uncertainty.

But the trader who thinks like a sniper knows this: your edge is not just the setup; your edge is your certainty in **execution.**

This chapter is a meditation on the power of single-minded execution. It's about cultivating a level of preparedness and inner trust so deep that when the setup appears, there is no emotional noise, no panic, no paralysis. Only one action. One shot. One clean decision. And the full weight of your preparation behind it.

Why Hesitation Kills Execution

"You don't rise to the level of your intentions - you fall to the level of your training."

In trading, hesitation is the invisible enemy. It slips in unnoticed. It disguises itself as caution, as prudence, as "being sure." But it is none of those things.

Hesitation, in the moment of trade execution, is simply a reflection of **incomplete preparation and mental fragmentation**.

The sniper doesn't hesitate because:

- He already knows his shot before he ever gets into position.
- He has simulated the scenario in his mind, again and again.
- He does not wait for certainty - he trusts the plan he has built and rehearsed.

The undisciplined trader hesitates because:

- He's watching the market **to find something**, not waiting for what he already knows.
- He has too many variables and not enough clarity.
- His confidence is derived from recent wins and external cues, not from internal structure.

Hesitation shows up in subtle ways:

- A delay in placing a trade that causes a missed entry

- A desire to "wait for one more candle" out of fear

- A reluctance to size up when your edge is strong

- A freeze when price reaches your stop - and you start rationalising why you shouldn't exit

This hesitation is the mental equivalent of a shaky trigger finger. In high-stakes environments - whether on the battlefield or in the markets - it leads to failure, not because of poor tools, but because of poor trust.

To eliminate hesitation, we must stop trying to be perfect and start being **prepared**. The trade should already be decided **before** the price reaches your level. The decision is not made in real-time. It is made long before - and execution is simply **honouring the decision**.

Rules-Based Trading as a Confidence Enhancer

"Confidence doesn't come from being right. It comes from being consistent."

Confidence is a paradox. The more we seek it from external outcomes - profits, praise, results - the more fragile it becomes. The more we build it from within - through process, structure, and integrity - the more unshakeable it becomes.

The sniper does not gain confidence from how many targets he has hit. He gains it from **how religiously he follows his process**.

In trading, the same applies.

A rules-based system is not a restriction - it is your liberation. It frees you from indecision, from emotional contamination, and from the exhausting loop of "should I or shouldn't I?"

The purpose of rules is to:

- **Define conditions clearly**: A trade is either valid or invalid. No grey area.

- **Limit emotional interference**: Your feelings don't get to vote. Only the data does.

- **Allow for post-trade clarity**: You can now evaluate success based on **process**, not just outcome.

- **Scale confidence over time**: Each disciplined execution, win or lose, deepens your belief in the system.

Imagine a sniper who questions the scope, wind, and bullet type every time he lines up a target. He wouldn't last a day. His equipment is tuned. His method is fixed. When he pulls the trigger, it is not based on a hunch - it is a mechanical response to a known pattern.

Rules create **mental automation**. That's what traders need more than anything - the ability to act decisively without emotional resistance.

Without rules, every trade becomes a psychological war. With rules, every trade becomes an act of obedience to your preparation.

Commitment to Your System

"The system does not work because it always wins. The system works because you always follow it."

Many traders build systems. Few stay loyal to them. They build the frame - then abandon it the moment discomfort arises. They override stops. They skip entries. They cherry-pick setups. And then, when results deteriorate, they question the system - not their inconsistency.

The sniper has no such luxury. He either follows protocol or risks mission failure. There is no glory in improvisation. There is only the mission - and the commitment to complete it with precision.

To master trading, you must reach the point where **your rules are law**, not guidelines.

You no longer trade "off-feel." You execute based on defined parameters.

You don't change your plan mid-trade. You act as a professional - deliberate, not reactive.

You know when to trade and when to sit out. Patience becomes an ally, not a punishment.

And most importantly - you accept the result **either way**. Because your goal is not to be right. Your goal is to be **consistent**. The wins and losses belong to the market. But your execution - that belongs to you. That is your responsibility. That is your edge.

There is a moment - just before the shot - when the sniper exhales. He quietens every voice, stills every movement, and lets go of all hesitation. In that breath, there is only now. Only alignment. Only trust.

This is the sacred space from which every elite trade must be executed.

When the market aligns with your rules...

When the setup you've defined presents itself...

When your plan signals it is time...

There must be no flinch. No fear. No noise.

There must only be action.

One shot. One kill.

That is the trader you are becoming.

SECTION TWO

Execution without emotion, entries without noise

5. Defining Your Kill Zone

How to Identify High-Probability Setups

The difference between a professional trader and an impulsive one is stark-just as the difference between a trained sniper and a chaotic foot soldier. While the latter may engage the enemy at the first sign of movement, the former waits-silently, patiently, immovably-until the moment is perfect. The sniper's kill zone is not merely a space; it is a carefully engineered opportunity. Defined with methodical precision, it is the convergence of preparation, clarity, and environment. Similarly, the trader's kill zone is not simply a chart pattern or a trendline-it is a **strategic moment of alignment**, where technical, structural, psychological, and probabilistic elements fuse together to form a high-probability setup.

This chapter is not about *what to trade*-it is about **when to strike**. It is about dissecting the battlefield with calm eyes, understanding the terrain, calculating the trajectory, and choosing that single shot that delivers disproportionate impact. In trading terms, it means only executing trades when **the odds are demonstrably in your favour**. Anything else is noise.

Risk-to-Reward Zones – The Geometry of Asymmetry

In the field, a sniper takes no unnecessary risks. The exposure must always be minimal, the objective precise, and the payoff decisive. This mirrors the trader's need to build every trade around one core principle: **favourable risk-to-reward**. It is the essence of strategic asymmetry. It ensures that over time, even a modest win rate can yield exponential results if the reward on the winners dwarfs the losses on the losers.

But favourable risk-to-reward is not wishful thinking. It must be derived from observable reality-**measurable levels, confirmed structure, and contextual backing**.

Defining the Parameters

1. **The Entry Point**: This is your firing position. It must be optimal-not just because price looks good, but because it is strategically aligned with technical and contextual criteria. Enter too early, and you expose your capital unnecessarily. Enter too late, and you sacrifice edge.

2. **The Stop-Loss**: This is your fallback point-the line that must not be crossed. It protects you from being emotionally dragged into a losing position. Like the sniper's cover, it defines the boundary between discipline and disaster.

3. **The Target Zone**: This is not a dream price. It is a calculated objective based on:
   - Previous swing highs/lows
   - Measured moves or price patterns
   - Fibonacci projections
   - Volume-based resistance/supply areas

The objective is not just to identify a reward that is larger than your risk, but to ensure that the *probability of reaching it* justifies the trade.

Dynamic Risk-to-Reward Thinking

A sniper constantly reassesses wind, range, and terrain. Similarly, traders must learn to adjust risk parameters based on **volatility, momentum, and broader market rhythm**. During periods of increased volatility, a wider stop may be necessary, but it must still be accompanied by a proportionately wider target. Likewise, in low-volatility conditions, tighter stops with conservative targets may serve better.

The art lies in creating a **zone**-a price window in which the entry, the stop, and the target are defined with clarity. The trade must make sense in **mathematical terms** (favourable R:R), in **psychological terms** (no fear of holding the position), and in **structural terms** (not fighting trend or liquidity).

This is your kill zone. It is not just where the trade *might* work-it is where the trade *must* work, or you're out.

Technical Confluences – When Signals Align Like Crosshairs

One of the defining traits of elite snipers is their ability to filter noise from signal. They are trained not to trust isolated data but to wait for *multiple confirmations*-factors that independently validate each other, creating a layered assurance of outcome.

In trading, this translates into **technical confluence**-the art of identifying zones where **multiple independent technical factors converge**. A single moving average crossover or candlestick pattern means little in isolation. But when several tools point to the same conclusion, your probability soars.

Examples of Powerful Confluence in the Kill Zone

1. **Trend Confluence Across Timeframes**

   - When the **daily**, **weekly**, and **monthly** charts all exhibit a bullish configuration-e.g., price above the 200 EMA, higher highs and higher lows, or ascending channels-this creates a multi-layered validation.

   - This is akin to the sniper having confirmation from multiple observation posts before proceeding.

2. **Indicator Agreement**

   - A **MACD crossover**, a **Super Trend confirmation**, and a **bullish engulfing candle** forming on the same zone do not happen randomly.

   - When independent indicators-each derived from different principles-align, their message carries weight.

3. **Structural and Pattern-Based Overlap**

   - If a price level is simultaneously:

     o A Fibonacci retracement level,

     o A prior resistance-turned-support,

     o A neckline of an inverse head and shoulders,

- o And a psychological round number (say 1000), then that price area demands attention. It is where **price memory** and **market psychology** intersect.

4. **Volume Confirmation**

- No shot is complete without accounting for commitment. In the market, volume shows intent.

- A breakout with strong volume is the difference between a whisper and a roar. It confirms that the market agrees with your thesis.

Confluence creates conviction. It doesn't guarantee success- but it significantly tilts the odds in your favour. For the sniper, the moment to shoot is when distance, wind, sight alignment, and breathing are all in sync. For the trader, the moment to enter is when price, structure, indicator, and context say the same thing.

Context, Structure, and Confirmation – The Intelligence Behind the Execution

If technical confluence is your weapon, **context is your battlefield intelligence**. No sniper would position himself without understanding the terrain-visibility, elevation, enemy presence, potential escape routes. Similarly, no trader should isolate a chart from its broader market environment.

Context: The Macro and Sectoral Backdrop

- What is the overall market doing?

- Are global indices in risk-on or risk-off mode?

- Is the sector leading or lagging the broader index?

- Are there macroeconomic events or earnings that could cause distortion?

A good setup in a bad context is like an ambush in fog-you may have the right aim, but the result is uncertainty.

Structure: The Blueprint of Price Behaviour

- Where are the **major swing highs and lows**?
- Are you at a breakout, a breakdown, or a retest zone?
- Is the instrument forming a **consolidation**, **accumulation**, or **distribution** structure?

Structure tells you where the market has previously shown its hand. These are the places where the big players act-their footprints are embedded in support and resistance zones, trendlines, channels, and supply-demand clusters.

When your kill zone aligns with these structural areas, you're not hunting in the dark-you're positioning where the action historically concentrates.

Confirmation: The Final Green Light

A sniper may have a clear view, but he waits for the target to present itself fully-no partial silhouette, no guessing. Similarly, **confirmation in trading** is your final permission to act. It comes in many forms:

- A breakout followed by a successful retest and rejection of the old level
- A trendline break supported by volume

- A reversal candle at a zone of interest (e.g., pin bars, engulfing patterns)

- A MACD histogram flipping positive after a period of bearishness

Confirmation is not about certainty-but about increasing conviction. You don't shoot because you want to. You shoot because the environment confirms that the moment has arrived.

6. The Tools of the Trade

Indicators That Align with Precision

A sniper's success is not merely a function of his intent to eliminate the target-it is a symphony of tools, training, terrain awareness, and timing. He does not rely on instincts alone; he leans on instruments that enhance his vision, compensate for distortion, and measure the invisible variables of distance, pressure, and wind. Precision is not an accident. It is the outcome of discipline applied through tools used with purpose.

A trader who seeks mastery must approach the market with this same ethos. In a world saturated with charts, news, flashing signals, and self-proclaimed trading gurus, what separates the erratic from the elite is not more data-it is **disciplined filtration**. It is not more indicators-it is **fewer tools used masterfully**.

This chapter lays bare the truth about indicators. They do not predict. They do not guarantee. They guide. Used poorly, they confuse. Used wisely, they clarify. When employed with the discipline of a sniper, they do not distract-they direct. They become extensions of your perception, amplifying your ability to observe and execute with precision.

Let us now explore the minimalist, yet profoundly effective, indicator toolkit that aligns with the philosophy of the sniper-trader-**Super Trend, MACD, and EMAs**-and how each one plays a distinct, indispensable role in orchestrating clean, high-probability trades.

Your Core: Super Trend, MACD, EMAs

The objective is not to use many tools. The objective is to master the few that consistently deliver clarity without clutter. These core tools-Super Trend, MACD, and EMAs-represent a balanced trinity of trend, momentum, and structure.

They do not compete for attention. They complement one another, forming a triangulation system where each indicator fills a specific role in defining the trade's edge.

Each of these tools has been carefully selected not because of popularity, but because of their ability to work **in unison-**delivering confirmation across multiple dimensions of the market without overcomplicating the execution process.

Super Trend – The Tactical Overlay (The Laser Sight)

Super Trend is a trend-following overlay that uses the Average True Range (ATR) to calculate dynamic support and resistance zones based on price volatility. Its core value lies in its **visual simplicity** and its ability to **cut through short-term noise**.

Like a sniper's laser sight, Super Trend doesn't tell you whether to shoot-but it does help you align your shot. When price sits clearly above the Super Trend line across multiple timeframes, the market is confirming that you are on the right side of momentum.

Its purpose is two fold:

1. **Trend Confirmation** – Are you trading with or against the broader tide?

2. **Exit Guidance** – Has the prevailing structure been compromised?

Why it works:

- It adapts to volatility, making it dynamic rather than static.

- It prevents you from prematurely exiting trending trades.

- It visually confirms whether price is respecting directional bias.

Best practices in our framework:

- Entry consideration is valid only when price is **above the Super Trend line on the Daily, Weekly, and Monthly charts.**

- An exit is triggered when price closes **below the Super Trend line on the Weekly chart**, providing a slower, more reliable signal that allows trends to play out.

In essence, Super Trend eliminates ambiguity. It acts as a behavioural cue that reinforces patience when the trend is intact and warns of structural deterioration when the trend is waning.

MACD – The Momentum Decoder (The Wind Meter)

Price alone can deceive. A sniper never fires without accounting for wind-it is invisible, yet powerful enough to veer a bullet off course. Similarly, a trader must account for **momentum**-the force behind price.

The **MACD (Moving Average Convergence Divergence)** reveals this hidden dimension. It doesn't just reflect price action-it decodes the **strength, direction, and sustainability of that price movement**. It highlights the energy behind the move, offering early warnings of exhaustion or continuation.

MACD is constructed from the differential between two EMAs-typically 12 and 26-and compared against a 9-period signal line. But its power lies in interpretation, not its formula.

How MACD fits into the sniper strategy:

- **Momentum Alignment**: Only engage when MACD is aligned across all key timeframes (Daily, Weekly, Monthly). A bullish crossover of the MACD line above the Signal line confirms strength behind the move.

- **Divergence Warnings**: If price makes a new high but MACD doesn't-momentum is waning. This is your wind shift. It's a sign that continuation may be fragile or manipulated.

- **Histogram Analysis**: Watch the histogram bars. Increasing bars suggest momentum is growing. Fading bars warn of deceleration-valuable when managing trades or watching for exit zones.

MACD is not a trigger. It's a **contextual validator**. It ensures that when you pull the trigger, you do so with the wind at your back-not in your face.

EMAs – The Structural Backbone (The Range Finder)

While Super Trend refines entries and MACD measures flow, the **Exponential Moving Averages (EMAs)** serve as your **macro alignment system**-your long-range scanner, your range finder.

Used strategically, EMAs provide the **framework of trend structure**. They track the consensus of market participants over different time horizons. Our sniper framework uses three core EMAs:

- **50 EMA**: The short-term trend tracker. Reflects the behaviour of swing traders.

- **100 EMA**: The medium-term direction filter. Used by institutions to confirm stability.

- **200 EMA**: The long-term bias line. Widely respected by hedge funds, mutual funds, and algorithmic models.

These EMAs are applied specifically to the **Daily timeframe** to establish *whether the stock or index is structurally strong*. The ideal configuration for long setups is:

- Price > 50 EMA > 100 EMA > 200 EMA

This order signals that buyers are in control across all layers. It creates a bullish stack, where momentum is flowing smoothly through short, medium, and long-term traders alike.

The trader who ignores this alignment risks engaging when the battlefield is not in their favour. Without EMA alignment, the ground beneath your position is unstable.

How Each Tool Plays a Role – The Synergy of Precision Instruments

Just as a sniper's kit is more than a rifle, a trader's setup must function as a **system**-where each tool serves a defined purpose.

Let's reframe each indicator as a tactical tool:

- **Super Trend** is your **laser sight** – It keeps your attention locked on the target. It tracks direction with clarity and adjusts as volatility changes.

- **MACD** is your **wind meter** – It reads what you cannot see. It senses energy and movement, ensuring your shot is not pushed off course by hidden momentum shifts.

- **EMAs** are your **range finder** – They help you assess distance, structure, and trend layers. They define the battlefield and tell you whether you're in enemy territory or holding the high ground.

Used in isolation, each tool is helpful.

Used together, they become formidable.

The synergy between them transforms guesswork into geometry. It brings rhythm, balance, and precision to your execution. When all three align-when your laser is stable, the wind is calm, and the range is known-**you have the perfect shot.**

Keep It Lean, Keep It Clean – Simplicity is Superiority

The modern trader is flooded with temptation. Every charting platform offers dozens of indicators. Forums tout the latest "secret formula." Social media amplifies noise in the name of novelty.

But sophistication in trading is not about complication. It is about **refinement.**

The sniper's toolkit is minimal not because he lacks access to more-but because he values stealth, clarity, and efficiency. Every extra instrument is a liability. Every distraction is a potential error.

In trading, your edge comes not from how many indicators you deploy-but from how cleanly you interpret the few that matter. Cluttered charts create doubt. Doubt breeds hesitation. Hesitation leads to poor execution.

A chart with too many tools is like a sniper with four scopes mounted, two wind meters buzzing, and no clear line of sight. **He misses. Every time.**

Therefore:

- **Avoid indicator overlap**. Don't use multiple momentum tools or trend filters that tell you the same thing in slightly different ways.

- **Limit visual clutter**. Your brain processes visuals faster than text. If your chart looks chaotic, your decisions will mirror that chaos.

- **Trust your core system**. Once you have a proven, high-probability setup, *stop searching*. Sharpen it instead.

Simplicity is not the enemy of precision. It is its prerequisite.

7. The Trigger

Knowing Exactly When to Pull the Trigger

In the world of the elite sniper, the final act-the pull of the trigger-is not one of reaction, but of orchestration. It is not the climax of chaos but the culmination of calm. A single, fluid squeeze of the trigger comes only after hundreds of silent calculations: wind, distance, visibility, movement, and moment. The sniper does not shoot because he *can*-he shoots because he *must*. Because all conditions converge into an irrefutable truth: *this is the shot.*

Trading demands the same ethos. The market, like the battlefield, is full of false signals, fleeting movements, and noise disguised as opportunity. The undisciplined trader fires recklessly-chasing price, reacting to headlines, guessing entries. The sniper-trader waits, watches, and moves only when clarity arrives. And when it does, there is no hesitation. There is only execution.

This chapter explores the defining moment of transition-the trigger. Not just how to enter, but when. Not just based on a setup, but on the *alignment of conviction, context, and confirmation.* This is the art of knowing when a trade deserves to be taken-not from impulse, but from informed precision.

Entry Mechanics – The Art of Strategic Initiation

Precision begins with process. A sniper has a ritual before the shot. He aligns breath, posture, sight, and heart rate. The trader must do the same-not with bullets, but with **criteria**. A structured entry is not mechanical-it is *methodical*. It allows you to act without second-guessing.

1. Structure First, Signal Later

A sniper never points his rifle at shadows. Similarly, a trade is only valid when it is built on a *defined structure*. Before any entry is even considered, certain baseline conditions must be met.

- **Trend Structure**: Price must be above the 200 EMA on the Daily chart. This signals alignment with institutional flows.

- **EMA Configuration**: 50 EMA > 100 EMA > 200 EMA on the Daily. This creates bullish flow from short- to long-term holders.

- **Super Trend Confirmation**: Price above Super Trend (5,1) on Daily, Weekly, and Monthly timeframes.

- **MACD Momentum**: MACD line above Signal line on all three timeframes. This confirms that the move is not just directional but supported by force.

This is your kill zone. You are no longer reacting-you are now preparing to engage.

2. The Trigger Candle – The Final Green Light

Within your kill zone, the final signal to pull the trigger must come from **price itself**. The candle is the heartbeat of the market-it tells the story of fear and conviction in real time.

Ideal trigger candles include:

- **Bullish Engulfing**: A wide-range candle that engulfs the previous bar, ideally at the breakout point or after a pullback.

- **Breakout Candle**: A candle that closes decisively above a well-defined resistance.

- **Reversal Candle**: A hammer or pin bar forming at support after a pullback within a trend.

Conditions for the trigger candle:

- Closes higher than it opens (bullish bias).

- Closes near its high (minimal upper wick).

- Supported by rising volume (especially if breaking resistance).

- Forms within a pre-defined structural zone-not randomly in space.

The sniper does not shoot at every movement. He pulls the trigger only when the target enters the crosshairs and stands still. Your trigger candle is that stillness-*momentary but telling*.

3. Enter at the Close – Not in Anticipation

Too many traders make the fatal error of anticipating confirmation before it is real. They act at the sight of green, not at the close of strength. But an unfinished candle is like a blurry target. It can change shape before it settles.

A disciplined sniper waits for clarity. Similarly, enter only **after the candle has closed**, with the confirmation locked in. If the candle fails to close strong, the setup is no longer valid. Let it go. There will always be another shot.

4. Risk Anchored in Structure

Where you enter matters. But where you exit if wrong matters more. A proper stop-loss is not emotional-it is structural.

- **Option 1**: Just below the low of the trigger candle.
- **Option 2**: Below the most recent swing low or support zone.

Never use a fixed-point stop (e.g., "2% below entry"). It must respect structure and volatility. Your stop defines where your thesis fails-not where your patience does.

5. Position Sizing – Risk Comes First

Never let enthusiasm dictate the size of your position. The sniper doesn't shoot bigger bullets because he's more excited. The size of the trade should be a function of your account size and your predefined risk per trade-*not your emotions*.

Multi-Timeframe Confirmation – Stacking the Odds in Your Favour

Snipers never act on a single lens. They consult scopes, satellites, and intelligence feeds. They see the landscape in layers.

So must the trader. A setup that looks clean on the Daily may be contradictory to the Weekly or ambiguous on the Monthly. A true high-probability trade aligns across all timeframes. This alignment doesn't just increase probability-it reduces uncertainty. And uncertainty is the enemy of decisive execution.

1. Monthly – The Strategic Sentiment

The Monthly chart is your compass. It doesn't provide entries-it provides orientation. A bullish Monthly candle tells you that long-term capital is flowing in. If the candle is green, wide-ranged, and making higher highs, it shows participation from investors-not just short-term traders.

Use Monthly Super Trend, MACD, and price action to identify if the macro bias is aligned. You're not looking to enter based on Monthly, but to validate that you're not shooting against the storm.

2. Weekly – The Tactical Context

This is the intermediate zone. Here, we assess:

Are we in a weekly uptrend or correction?

Is the Weekly Super Trend supportive?

Has the Weekly MACD flipped bullish?

The Weekly chart should not contradict the Monthly-it should refine it. It gives you rhythm. If the Weekly candle is forming a base, a breakout, or a higher low, and aligns with momentum, you're nearing your moment of engagement.

3. Daily – The Execution Frame

The Daily chart is where the shot is taken. All analysis points here. This is where:

Your entry is triggered by price action.

Your stop is placed based on candle structure.

Your risk and position sizing are finalised.

Only when **all three timeframes** align-Monthly macro, Weekly structure, Daily confirmation-do you have a setup worth acting on.

This is how professionals build confidence: not by guessing, but by synchronising.

8. Escape Plan

Exiting with Precision and Preserving Capital

A sniper's success is not measured by the sound of the bullet leaving the chamber-it is measured by whether he gets home. The shot is not the end of the story; it is merely the midpoint. What follows is equally, if not more, critical: the *exfiltration-* the clean exit, without noise, without trace, without regret.

So it is in trading.

Entry may receive the glory, but **exit defines the outcome**. A perfect setup, executed flawlessly, can still end in failure if the exit is undisciplined, delayed, or emotionally driven. Too many traders obsess over entries and ignore exits, treating them as an afterthought rather than a strategic imperative. But exits are not the backdoor of a trade-they are the *final, conscious act of professional decision-making*. And they must be treated with the same surgical focus as the entry.

This chapter is about the often-overlooked skill of knowing when to disengage. Not when it's convenient. Not when it feels good. But when the **conditions for staying are no longer valid**, or when the **target has been reached**. The sniper-trader does not wait for perfection. He moves with purpose and exits with precision-because he understands that *preserving capital is survival*, and survival is the basis of longevity.

Exit Criteria – Pre-defined, Not Improvised

A sniper never improvises his exit strategy mid-mission. The plan is set before the rifle is even chambered. The path in is tied to the path out. This is not rigidity-it is clarity. In trading, your exit must be *structured, rule-based, and predefined* before the trigger is pulled.

To trade without a pre-set exit plan is to shoot and hope. It is to gamble, not operate.

Why Most Traders Fail at Exits

- **They rely on emotion**: Greed for more gains, fear of losing profit, hesitation in locking in success.

- **They act reactively**: Making decisions based on price movement in isolation, rather than a broader strategy.

- **They treat exits as afterthoughts**: Obsessing over entries, ignoring the importance of controlled disengagement.

To avoid these traps, exits must be planned along three axes:

1. **Profit-target based** (where the shot hits),

2. **Structural breakdown-based** (when the terrain shifts),

3. **Time-based** (when opportunity costs begin to outweigh patience).

Let's examine these more deeply.

1. Exit at Target – Precision Hits

This is the cleanest type of exit. A sniper doesn't linger after the shot hits the mark. In trading, this means setting a **predefined target level** where you will take profits-no questions asked.

How to determine targets:

- **Previous swing highs/lows** (horizontal resistance or support)
- **Measured move projections** (using the size of a range or pattern)
- **Fibonacci extensions** (commonly 1.618, 2.0 levels)
- **Round number psychology** (e.g., 1000, 1500, etc.)

These levels must be realistic, not greedy. The target must make sense within the structure of the trade-not just based on hope or a percentage goal.

The sniper does not shoot at multiple targets at once. He has **one objective, one shot, one extraction.** So should the trader.

2. Exit on Structural Breakdown – Aborting the Mission

No plan survives contact with the market. Conditions evolve. What looked like a promising setup can morph into risk. The market starts speaking a different language-and if you don't exit, you stay to fight a battle you never intended to enter.

Structural exits are based on **deterioration of the setup**. Not based on fear. Not based on a red candle. But based on *invalidated context.*

Examples of structural deterioration:

- Price closes below the Super Trend (5,1) on the **Weekly** timeframe (our primary trailing tool).

- Price closes below a key moving average (e.g., 50 EMA or 100 EMA).

- MACD crosses against your position across multiple timeframes.

- Bearish engulfing candle forms near resistance with volume spike.

- Higher lows or higher highs fail to form-signalling potential trend exhaustion.

This is the equivalent of the sniper seeing incoming threats, or the weather shifting mid-mission. He doesn't fight it. He exits. Lives to shoot another day.

3. Exit Based on Time – Opportunity Cost Management

One of the most deceptive threats to a trader's capital is not loss-it is stagnation. A sniper who lingers too long is exposed. A trader who holds too long in dead money trades burns mental bandwidth, time, and opportunity.

A position that is going nowhere *is going somewhere*-just not in your favour.

Time-based exit examples:

- Price remains range-bound or directionless for more than **8–10 trading sessions** post entry.

- No volume confirmation or trend follow-through within **2 trading weeks**.

- Volatility contracts significantly, rendering the trade inefficient.

This kind of exit is strategic, not emotional. It's an acknowledgment that **time is capital**. And that idle capital in a drifting trade is a form of invisible loss.

Trailing Stops and Time-Based Exits – Tools That Think for You

Even the best snipers don't manually calculate every variable on the fly. They rely on calibrated instruments that track for them. Trailing stops and time-based exits are your operational assistants. They preserve profits, reduce overthinking, and build consistency.

Trailing Stops – Locking In, Not Giving Back

A trailing stop allows you to stay in a winning trade for as long as the trend remains valid, while ensuring that a reversal doesn't erase your gains.

In our sniper-trading methodology, the **Weekly Super Trend (5,1)** acts as a trailing stop:

- As long as price closes above the Super Trend line on the **Weekly** timeframe, the trade is held.

- A close below it triggers a **discipline-based exit**, not a discretionary one.

This method avoids:

- Exiting too early.

- Getting shaken out by intraday noise.

- Letting profit turn into loss.

Other trailing methods *(to be used selectively)*:

- **Swing low trailing**: Move stop below each higher low in an uptrend.

- **ATR trailing**: Use a multiple of the ATR value to adjust stops dynamically.

- **Fixed-percentage trail**: After every 5% move, shift stop 3% higher.

The point is not the method-it's the **execution of the method**. Let it do the thinking. Trust it. Honour it.

Time-Based Exits – Cut the Cord

Every trade should come with a ticking clock. If the expected outcome hasn't materialised in a predefined window, exit. This applies even if the trade is slightly profitable. Why?

Because:

- It's draining focus from better setups.

- It keeps capital captive in mediocrity.

- It creates emotional drag.

A sniper does not stay perched once the window of opportunity has passed. He packs up and relocates. You should too.

Protecting Gains Like Your Life Depends on It

There's a dangerous psychology that afflicts successful traders-it's the illusion of invincibility. A few wins, and suddenly the rules seem optional. Stops get moved. Targets get stretched. Risks creep in.

This is when the sniper-trader reminds himself: **your profit is not yours until it's protected**.

Protecting Gains Is a Code, Not a Choice

- **Paper profits are not real profits**
  - Until you exit, that 10% gain is fiction. Don't be seduced by numbers on a screen.

- **Never let a winner become a loser**
  - If a trade is up more than 5%, move your stop to breakeven or higher.
  - Losing money after being ahead is not just financial-it's psychological damage.

- **Partial profits = emotional buffer**
  - Exit 50–70% at target.
  - Let the remainder ride with a trailing stop.
  - You de-risk and de-stress the trade while keeping upside open.

- **Respect the parabolic**

- o If price explodes irrationally in your favour, *don't freeze*. Book partials aggressively.
- o Markets that give you 30% in 3 days can take it back in 3 minutes.

The Mental Edge of Exiting Well

When you exit with clarity:

- **You avoid regret.**
- **You reinforce your system.**
- **You build confidence, not confusion.**

The sniper doesn't shoot emotionally. He doesn't escape chaotically. He follows the code. So must you.

63

SECTION THREE

The Sniper's Discipline

9. Avoiding Overtrading

Why Spray-and-Pray Is a Losing Game

The battlefield of trading is strewn with the wreckage of traders who pulled the trigger too often, too soon, and too emotionally. Much like a soldier without a mission, many traders fall into the trap of overactivity - not because they lack skill, but because they lack stillness. In trading, as in sniping, it is not the frequency of action that determines mastery, but the *quality* and *intention* behind each decision. Overtrading is the trader's equivalent of spray-and-pray – an impulsive and indiscriminate attempt to "catch something" in the market, driven more by anxiety and craving than by clarity and conviction.

This chapter delves deep into the psychological, emotional, and strategic dynamics that fuel overtrading. We examine how the neurochemical underpinnings of desire hijack decision-making, how emotional reaction displaces disciplined execution, and how forced trades become silent saboteurs of long-term performance. In doing so, we realign our approach to embody the discipline of a sniper: calm, calculated, and patient - choosing *when not to trade* as deliberately as when to act.

Dopamine Traps in Trading

Modern trading platforms are engineered not only to execute trades but to stimulate the mind. The flashing green and red candles, the ticking price quotes, the real-time P&L swings -

all of it creates a sensory playground for the human brain. Behind the allure of this digital battlefield lies a powerful neurochemical driver: **dopamine**.

Dopamine, contrary to popular belief, is not about reward itself. It is about the *anticipation* of reward. This subtle but crucial distinction reveals why trading can so easily become addictive. The possibility of making money, of catching the next breakout, or of being "right" in a fast-moving market lights up the same neural circuits associated with gambling, gaming, and even substance dependence.

For traders, this means that the mere act of *watching* the market triggers a dopamine loop. Every time a chart pattern forms, or a news alert pops up, dopamine is released - urging the trader to take action. It whispers, *"There might be something here... don't miss it."* Over time, this biochemical conditioning distorts the trader's ability to assess setups rationally. The pursuit of *high-quality trades* gets replaced by a craving for *any trade*.

It is not uncommon for traders caught in this loop to justify poor decisions with false logic. *"It might bounce from here,"* or *"I'll just take a small position,"* become post-facto rationalisations for dopamine-driven impulses. What appears on the surface to be a technical or strategic move is often nothing more than a neurochemical reaction dressed in trader's clothing.

To think like a sniper is to be acutely aware of this trap. A sniper doesn't aim at shadows or react to every sound in the forest. They *observe*, they *breathe*, and they *wait* - unmoved by noise, unmoved by the compulsion to act without cause. The disciplined trader must do the same. By recognising the source of our urges, we can detach from them. Dopamine need not be our enemy, but it must never become our commander.

Systematic Execution vs. Emotional Reaction

Imagine a sniper who discards their rangefinder, ignores wind speed, and starts firing because "it feels right." They would not last a day on the field. Precision depends on *process*, not on passion. The same principle applies in trading. Execution without a system is not trading - it is gambling.

Systematic execution is the hallmark of a trader who has transcended emotion. It means having a well-defined strategy, knowing *exactly* what conditions must be present to initiate a trade, and having the patience to wait until those conditions are met - no matter how long it takes. It also means knowing your risk before you enter, your exit before you begin, and your response to every possible outcome. In short, it is the disciplined practice of *preparation before participation*.

Emotional reaction, on the other hand, is rooted in insecurity. It is the voice that says, *"I need to make something happen."* It thrives in the absence of structure. The trader who reacts emotionally often finds themselves entering trades without a clear edge, sizing positions based on fear or greed, and exiting either too early or too late - not because their system told them to, but because their *feelings* took over.

Overtrading often begins where process ends. The emotional trader feels compelled to "do something" after a missed opportunity, a losing streak, or even a moment of boredom. Their actions become erratic, their edge becomes diluted, and their confidence begins to erode. What they fail to realise is that each emotionally reactive trade takes them further away from the consistent execution they claim to seek.

In contrast, the sniper operates from *control*. They are unhurried, unbothered by missed chances, and uninterested in proving anything. They only pull the trigger when their checklist aligns, when their environment supports the shot, and when all variables have been accounted for. This is not passivity - it is *measured aggression.*

To trade like a sniper is to trade with intentionality. Your system becomes your spotter - guiding, filtering, and protecting you from impulsive error. Without a system, every trade is a shot in the dark. With a system, every shot is calibrated, purposeful, and aligned with your higher goal: long-term precision and profit.

The Cost of Forced Trades

Perhaps the most dangerous trades a trader can make are those they *know* they shouldn't. These are the trades taken out of frustration, revenge, boredom, or desperation - what we call *forced trades.* Though they may seem harmless in isolation, their cumulative cost is immense.

Let's examine the hidden damages:

i. Emotional Cost

Every forced trade chips away at the trader's emotional capital. It breeds self-doubt, regret, and inconsistency. Even if the trade results in profit, it leaves behind a residue of anxiety. Why? Because the trader knows deep down it wasn't aligned with their process. Over time, this inner conflict creates hesitation - the kind that causes missed opportunities and flawed decision-making when it matters most.

ii. Opportunity Cost

Capital deployed on low-probability trades is capital that is unavailable for *high-probability* setups. This is particularly damaging for sniper-style traders, who rely on selectivity. The trader may miss the ideal trade because they are already locked into a poor position, mentally and financially. The market punishes the impatient by making them *unavailable* when the real opportunity arises.

iii. Financial Cost

While one or two poor trades might not derail a portfolio, a pattern of forced trades can. The accumulation of transaction costs, slippage, drawdowns, and misallocated risk adds up. And when losses mount from trades that had no reason to be placed in the first place, the psychological damage multiplies.

iv. Habitual Cost

This may be the most dangerous of all. When forced trades are occasionally rewarded - due to randomness or luck - they create reinforcement of bad behaviour. The brain begins to associate emotional, unplanned action with positive outcomes, encouraging the trader to repeat the mistake. What starts as a one-off impulse becomes a habitual pattern. The sniper becomes a cowboy, and precision becomes collateral damage.

Forced trades dilute discipline. They feed ego, not equity. They are emotionally satisfying in the moment but strategically devastating over time.

The disciplined trader, like the seasoned sniper, learns to hold fire. They are comfortable doing nothing when there is nothing to do. They do not need the market to provide constant stimulation. They seek quality over quantity, clarity over chaos.

In a world where overactivity is often confused with ambition, it takes a rare kind of strength to wait. To resist the urge to act for action's sake. To trade with precision instead of passion. To let go of the need to be constantly engaged - and instead, be selectively lethal.

The sniper does not spray bullets. The sniper waits for the shot that matters. So too must the trader.

Overtrading is not a sign of dedication - it is a sign of disconnection from process, from purpose, and from patience. And every trade that is not born of clarity is a step away from mastery.

10. Staying Invisible

Emotional Stealth and Tactical Silence

There is a certain elegance in invisibility. A certain power in remaining untraceable. The sniper knows this better than anyone. His craft depends on silence, his edge is drawn from restraint, and his survival is secured through discretion. He is neither seen nor heard - but when the time is right, he strikes with devastating precision. He doesn't need to be noticed to be effective. He needs to be aligned, focused, and above all - **unseen**.

In trading, the same ethos applies. The markets are filled with noise, with bravado, with constant declarations of certainty and prediction. Social feeds light up with positions and profits, traders clamour for recognition, and opinions swing louder than price itself. But the trader who operates like a sniper does not participate in this theatre. They embrace **emotional stealth**, **strategic anonymity**, and **tactical silence** - because they know that visibility can be a liability, and validation can become a trap.

This chapter explores how invisibility - mental, emotional, and operational - can offer one of the most profound edges in the trading world. We'll delve into the psychology of silent execution, the toxicity of external noise, and the quiet liberation that comes from keeping your process unseen and undisturbed.

Trade in Silence, Grow in Silence

The modern trader faces a unique temptation - the allure of being *seen*. We live in an era where success isn't just pursued; it is *performed*. Screenshots of profits, boasts of "perfect entries," and bold market calls are paraded across platforms, not as markers of mastery, but as bait for validation. Yet, what is gained in applause is often lost in *clarity*.

The sniper-trader follows a different doctrine: **operate in silence, evolve in solitude.**

Trading in silence is not merely about secrecy - it is about protection. It's about protecting your process from premature exposure. It's about guarding your emotional neutrality from the distortions of external opinion. And it's about cultivating confidence that does not depend on public affirmation.

Every time you share a trade publicly, you increase your attachment to the outcome. You're no longer managing the position objectively - you're managing your *image*. What happens if the trade fails? What if it hits your stop-loss? Do you still follow your exit plan, or do you delay, hoping to save face?

Silence removes this interference. It anchors you in *internal truth*, not external performance. It frees you from the need to explain, justify, or prove. And that freedom creates space - space to think clearly, to refine deeply, and to act with zero hesitation.

Growing in silence is even more sacred. It means you evolve without the pressure to demonstrate progress. It means you make mistakes, learn, improve - all behind closed doors. Like a seed that grows underground before it ever breaks the surface, the silent trader builds deep roots. They do not grow tall first. They grow strong.

Public growth often leads to performative growth - where the focus shifts from becoming better to appearing better. But real growth is messy, nonlinear, and unglamorous. It requires patience. It requires space. It requires silence.

The sniper doesn't train on the battlefield. He trains far from view, perfecting his art in obscurity. So does the trader. Mastery is a private affair. Results speak. Everything else whispers.

Reducing Noise: Social Media, Over-Analysis, and Herd Mentality

The market is not your only opponent. There is another, subtler enemy - one that resides in your ears, eyes, and fingertips. It is called *noise*. And in the information age, it is relentless.

Noise is the enemy of clarity.

It is not just misinformation. It is *excessive* information. It is the unfiltered opinions of others, the endless forecasts of pundits, the tweets of influencers, and the non-stop drumbeat of speculation. It is also the internal chaos created by too much analysis, too many indicators, and too much second-guessing.

Let's break this noise into its most invasive sources:

i. Social Media: The Theatre of Illusions

Social platforms are not built for trading. They are built for *attention*. And where attention is the currency, exaggeration becomes the norm. Most of what you see on social media is not strategy - it is theatre. The losses are hidden, the risks downplayed, the wins magnified.

A trader consuming this content consistently begins to doubt their own process. They chase someone else's conviction. They lose faith in their own setups. They start to believe that trading should be fast, flashy, and constant - when in fact, profitable trading is often slow, boring, and highly repetitive.

The sniper-trader unfollows the noise. Not out of arrogance, but out of necessity. Their clarity depends on it.

ii. Over-Analysis: When Intelligence Becomes Sabotage

Too much analysis is not a sign of diligence - it's a symptom of insecurity. It is the fear of being wrong, masked as "doing more homework." At a certain point, adding more indicators, more data, and more scenarios *reduces* clarity rather than enhances it.

Snipers don't calculate forever. They assess, confirm, and execute. Trading should be no different. Your edge lies in your system, not in your spreadsheet's complexity.

When you overanalyse, you paralyse. You wait for perfection. You wait for every signal to align perfectly, every piece of data to validate your idea. But markets don't wait. They reward those who are prepared, not those who are endlessly preparing.

Simplify. Strip your charts. Reduce your inputs. Focus only on the *essential*. That is how the sniper operates.

iii. Herd Mentality: The Death of Independent Thinking

The crowd is often loudest at the peak of greed and the depth of fear. When everyone is euphoric, the sniper-trader becomes cautious. When everyone panics, the sniper sharpens focus.

Herd mentality is comforting. It feels safe to agree with the majority. But in trading, *consensus is often the costliest place to be.*

A sniper doesn't shoot because others are shooting. He waits for his target. So should the trader. Let the herd run wild. Your job is not to run with them. Your job is to watch, to think, and to strike when *you* are ready - not when they are.

Reducing noise is not about being uninformed. It is about being *selectively informed*. It is about choosing inputs that serve your system, and discarding the rest. The quieter your mental space, the sharper your decision-making.

The Power of Anonymity in Strategy

Anonymity is often misunderstood. In a world obsessed with personal brands and public presence, staying anonymous can seem like a weakness. But to the sniper-trader, anonymity is not just a style - it is a strategic weapon.

When no one knows what you're trading, how you're trading, or why you're trading - you're free. Free to adapt. Free to evolve. Free to act without being cornered by the weight of past predictions or public opinions.

Let's explore how anonymity protects your edge:

i. Emotional Autonomy

Publicly declaring your trades ties your emotional wellbeing to the outcome. If it wins, you feel validated. If it loses, you feel exposed. Either way, your objectivity is compromised.

Private execution, on the other hand, allows you to operate without emotional pressure. You're not trying to prove anything. You're not trying to impress anyone. You're simply following your process.

ii. Strategic Flexibility

When you go public with a market call - say, "I'm long Tesla" - you create an identity attachment. Now, if the trade goes against you, it's not just a financial loss. It feels like a personal contradiction. You may delay exiting just to avoid admitting you were wrong. That hesitation can be fatal.

The sniper doesn't tell the enemy where he's hiding. He doesn't announce where he'll shoot from. His advantage lies in unpredictability.

So too with trading. An anonymous strategy is an adaptive strategy.

iii. Mental Clarity and Self-Reliance

By keeping your trading plan private, you reinforce self-reliance. You stop seeking others' approval. You learn to trust your research, your system, and your rules.

Anonymity fosters purity of process. No external distortion. No need to fit in. Just clean, clear execution.

The most powerful trades are often the ones no one knew you made - not because they were secret, but because they were undisturbed. That is the strength of invisibility.

There is a discipline in silence that very few understand. It is not emptiness - it is deliberate stillness. It is not disengagement - it is focused disengagement from distraction. It is not isolation - it is freedom from interference.

The sniper-trader doesn't crave attention. They crave alignment. They don't need to announce their skill - they express it in the silence of perfect execution. They aren't looking for applause - they're looking for accuracy.

To be invisible in this world is to be powerful beyond measure.

Trade without noise.

Grow without announcement.

And strike when no one sees it coming.

11. Breathing Through Chaos

Tactical Emotional Control

There comes a moment in every trader's journey - a point of high tension, deep uncertainty, or crushing loss - when the mind begins to spiral and composure begins to unravel. It's in these exact moments that the market reveals who is trained... and who is triggered.

Just as a sniper must maintain poise while staring down his scope under enemy fire, a trader must remain calm while staring at a fast-moving chart, an open loss, or a volatile news reaction. The difference between panic and precision is not knowledge. It is nervous system regulation. It is the ability to breathe through chaos, to remain emotionally undisturbed even as the external environment spins into disorder.

This chapter is a deep dive into the inner workings of psychological composure. It explores how snipers build stress immunity, how traders can borrow from those principles to operate under duress, and why true mastery begins not with what you do in calm - but with how you respond in chaos.

Handling Slippage, Losses, and Near-Misses

For the untrained trader, chaos is personal. But for the sniper-trader, chaos is **predictable**. And because it is expected, it is *prepared for*. This preparation is especially critical when dealing with the three most emotionally destabilising trading events: **slippage**, **losses**, and **near-misses.**

Slippage: The Shock of Reality vs Expectation

Slippage is the experience of not getting the price you planned for - and the psychological damage isn't in the points lost, but in the *loss of control*. When you've done your analysis, placed your stop or limit, and still receive a worse fill due to market volatility or thin liquidity, the immediate response is often disbelief: *"This shouldn't have happened."*

But the sniper-trader knows: the moment you enter the market, *you surrender a degree of control*. Execution is a partnership between your preparation and market conditions. Slippage is the market's fine print.

To master it:

- Use wider stops in volatile conditions or during event risks.

- Avoid low-liquidity trades where your exit could become the next candle.

- Accept a small margin of variability in outcome - just as a sniper accounts for shifting wind.

Remember, it's not the event - it's the reaction. If slippage makes you chase or revenge trade, the real damage has just begun.

Losses: The Emotional Cost of Doing the Right Thing

Few things are harder to accept than a loss that followed your plan to the letter. The setup was there. The risk was controlled. The entry was clean. And yet, the market went the other way. This triggers one of the most painful emotional responses in trading: **questioning your system** after a valid execution.

This is where amateurs retreat and overcorrect. They begin tweaking their strategy unnecessarily, widening stops, altering entry criteria - not because the system is broken, but because their **emotions are unprocessed**.

The sniper-trader does not see every bullet that misses as a failure. He knows that the variables are numerous - he controls what he can and releases the rest. So should the trader.

Every strategy has variance. A losing trade, even a series of them, may simply be part of that curve.

To deal with losses:

- Perform a *post-trade breakdown*, not a breakdown. Separate emotional reaction from procedural review.

- Assess: Was this a *bad outcome from a good decision*? If so, honour it.

- Detach your self-worth from your P&L. You are a *process executor*, not a fortune teller.

Near-Misses: The Mental Torture of Almost

The chart nearly hit your target and reversed. Or worse - it missed your entry by a tick before taking off. These are the near-misses that haunt traders, often far more than losses. Why? Because they feed the illusion of *"what could have been"*. The brain begins to play games: *"If only I had used a market order"*, *"Why did I hesitate?"*, *"This was my chance."*

These mental loops are not just distracting - they are **dangerous**. They pull you out of neutrality and into emotional logic. Soon you start altering your risk plan to avoid future regrets. You begin chasing to "make up" for what you missed.

The sniper-trader accepts that not every target aligns. A gust of wind, a shift in timing, an unexpected movement - it happens. He doesn't chase the ghost. He resets and waits again.

The path forward:

- Acknowledge the regret. Write it down. Then close the page.

- Review if your rules *were met*. If not, it's not your trade - it's just your ego reacting.

- Don't chase "the one that got away" by lowering standards for the next one.

Trading mastery is the art of moving on *without carrying emotional residue.*

How Snipers Train Their Nervous System

Emotional control is not willpower. It is **physiological training**. And elite snipers know this better than anyone. Their success depends on remaining still and composed in moments of extreme threat, pressure, and consequence. This is not a mental trick - it is the result of deliberate **nervous system conditioning**.

Let's explore how that discipline applies directly to the trader's chair.

Training Under Simulated Pressure

Snipers are exposed to stressful training scenarios repeatedly - loud noise, unexpected commands, multiple targets - all while being asked to maintain poise, timing, and accuracy. This repeated exposure builds a reflexive calm.

Traders must adopt a similar practice. During non-trading hours:

- Rehearse market scenarios that trigger you - sudden losses, open slippage, missed trades.

- Visualise the event in full sensory detail, but **rehearse a calm response**.

- Over time, the brain rewires itself to see the scenario as *expected*, not *threatening*.

This is *mental fortification* - building resilience before the battle begins.

Breathing as a Tactical Weapon

Breath is the sniper's anchor. When stress begins to rise, *the breath is the first system to lose control*. Shallow, fast breathing signals panic. Slow, deliberate breathing signals safety.

Tactical breathing techniques used by snipers (and applicable to traders):

- **Box Breathing**: Inhale (4s), hold (4s), exhale (4s), hold (4s) - repeat for 2–5 minutes.

- **1:2 Breathing Ratio**: Inhale for 4, exhale for 8 - shifts the body into parasympathetic recovery mode.

- **Reset Breath**: One full inhale through the nose, sighing exhale through the mouth - done three times during emotional volatility.

These techniques are not just stress management - they are **performance enablers**. They allow clarity to return, decisions to slow, and perspective to realign.

Body Awareness as a Signal

Snipers are trained to notice *micro-sensations* in the body - tightening of the jaw, twitch in the hand, breath held too long. These are precursors to emotional disruption. Traders should develop the same bodily awareness.

- Scan your body regularly during trading sessions.
- Catch the tension *before it drives impulsive action*.
- Use physical cues as feedback: If your breath is rushed or your shoulders are clenched - pause before you place the next order.

Stillness is not the absence of stress - it is the presence of internal command.

Techniques to Manage Cortisol and Stay Calm

Cortisol is not your enemy - but unmanaged, it becomes your saboteur. Elevated cortisol affects your cognition, sharpens your fear responses, narrows your focus to short-term threats, and weakens your decision-making. For the sniper-trader, *managing cortisol is mission-critical*.

i. Strategic Morning Priming

How you begin your day dictates your hormonal baseline. A cortisol spike in the morning (caused by emails, screens, or market chatter) sets a tone of agitation.

Instead:

- Begin your day with *stillness*.
- Use 5–10 minutes of breathwork, gentle stretching, or meditation.
- Avoid immediate exposure to financial media, WhatsApp messages, or Twitter sentiment.

Own your state before the market opens.

ii. The "Clear Space" Protocol

Build a *transition ritual* between trading blocks. After a trade, especially a loss, the nervous system holds tension. If you jump into the next setup, your perspective is still contaminated.

Use this reset between trades:

1. Stand up and walk for 90 seconds.
2. Deepen your breathing.
3. Journal a single sentence: *"That trade is complete. My state is clear."*

This tiny ritual resets both your body and mind. It tells the system: "That was one event - not a spiral."

iii. Environmental Control

Your environment either calms or stimulates your nervous system.

- Use dim, warm lighting to reduce adrenal stimulation.
- Minimise background tabs, pings, notifications.
- Keep water nearby and stay hydrated - dehydration elevates cortisol.
- Play ambient or instrumental music - known to reduce heart rate variability.

The sniper's room is sparse, focused, and quiet. So should be the trader's space. *Environment is energy.*

iv. Weekly Recovery Windows

Do not let trading become continuous arousal. Build a *day of full recovery*. No charts. No reviews. No market analysis. This is not laziness - it's **recalibration**.

Walk. Read. Train. Write. Restore.

Come back *sharpened*, not strained.

v. Sleep and Nutrition as Emotional Armour

You cannot regulate your emotions if your sleep is broken or your blood sugar is spiking.

- Prioritise 7–8 hours of sleep.
- Avoid caffeine or heavy meals late at night.

- Use magnesium or herbal support (under guidance) if sleep is fragmented.

Eat real, balanced food. Avoid sugar surges before trading sessions. Fuel your body like a professional - because **you are one.**

To breathe through chaos is to master the art of presence under pressure. It is to become the calm within the storm, the centred eye in the hurricane of volatility.

This chapter was not about theory. It was about training. Because in this business, the real weapon is not a system - it is a still nervous system.

And in a market filled with emotion, the trader who controls his own - wins.

.

12. Training Like a Marksman

Journaling, Backtesting, and Self-Correction

A marksman does not become precise by simply aiming. Precision is the result of **training, documentation, evaluation, and adjustment**. It's not about doing more - it's about doing better, again and again, with increasing awareness. The sniper understands this. Every round fired is recorded, analysed, deconstructed. He doesn't obsess over the shot - he obsesses over the process behind the shot.

The trader who thinks like a sniper brings the same level of *methodical reflection* to the charts. Winning trades aren't glorified, and losing trades aren't shamed - both are studied. Because in the end, trading mastery is not built in the moment of execution, but in the moments of **review and refinement**. What separates the seasoned trader from the novice is not just what they trade - it's how they *learn* from what they trade.

This chapter is dedicated to the discipline of training. Not in the theoretical sense, but in the deliberate, day-by-day practice of recording, reviewing, and recalibrating. Like the sniper's firing log, we explore how your trading journal becomes your most honest mentor. Like a mission debrief, we discuss the importance of trade reviews. And like a neural feedback loop, we dive into how real-time psychological calibration becomes your secret weapon.

The Sniper's Logbook: Your Trading Journal

The sniper's logbook is his blueprint. It is not simply a record of what happened - it is an account of *how*, *why*, and *under what conditions* each shot was taken. It captures not just the action, but the context: the weather, the terrain, the distance, the mindset, the breath control. These notes create a rich dataset from which patterns can be extracted, mistakes isolated, and edge enhanced.

Your trading journal is the same. It is not a diary. It is not a P&L statement. It is a **performance architecture** - a living document that reveals your habits, your weaknesses, your blind spots, and your hidden brilliance.

Why Most Traders Fail to Journal

Many traders skip journaling because they think it's time-consuming, unnecessary, or demotivating. But what they're really avoiding is **self-confrontation**. The journal is a mirror. It shows you exactly what happened - and that's uncomfortable when discipline has been breached.

But the sniper-trader does not seek comfort. He seeks truth. And the journal is where truth lives.

Structure of an Effective Journal

A journal must balance objectivity with introspection. It should be both quantitative and qualitative. Here's a deeply structured layout to follow:

Trade Metadata (Snapshot of the Setup)

- **Date & Time**
- **Instrument traded**
- **Timeframe**
- **Setup type / strategy trigger**
- **Entry Price**
- **Stop-Loss**
- **Target**
- **Position Size**
- **Result (P&L)**

This builds your database of trades. It's unemotional. Cold. Clean. Objective.

Execution Narrative (Context and Process)

- **Why was the trade entered?**
  - Which confluences were present?
  - Was it based on a system rule or an impulsive decision?
- **Was there hesitation or overconfidence?**
  - Did you enter early to "anticipate" the move?
  - Did you wait for confirmation or act on instinct?
- **How did you manage the trade?**
  - Did you trail the stop logically?
  - Did you let the trade hit target or interfere?

This section is where you begin to *read yourself* - not just the market.

Psychological Reflection (The Mind Behind the Trade)

- **What was my emotional state pre-trade?**
    - Calm, anxious, rushed, confident, distracted?
- **Did I follow my rules or make emotional decisions?**
    - Was there fear of missing out?
    - Was I revenge-trading after a loss?
- **How do I feel post-trade - and why?**
    - Regret, relief, pride, shame?

This is where you transform from trader to *student of behaviour*.

The sniper doesn't merely look at whether the bullet hit. He analyses whether *he was centred*, whether *his breath was steady*, whether *his judgment was sharp*. That's the mindset the journal builds.

Post-Mission Debriefs = Trade Reviews

When a sniper returns from a mission - whether successful or not - he sits down for a *debrief*. Every element of the mission is reviewed: timing, terrain, target movement, weapon mechanics, stress response. Even if the target was hit, the sniper still looks for ways to improve. Because the goal isn't to succeed once - it's to repeat that success under any conditions.

A trader must do the same. Trading is not a daily battle - it's a campaign. And the ability to deconstruct your trades consistently is what creates long-term advantage.

The Power of Pattern Recognition

A single trade tells you little. Ten trades tell you a story. Fifty trades show you *patterns*. You'll begin to see:

- That you often jump in too early on Monday mornings.
- That you exit too soon when trading large size.
- That you tend to skip trades after a loss, even if setups are valid.

These are not strategy flaws - they are **human tendencies**. Trade reviews bring them into the light.

Structure of a Trade Review Process

Daily Review: Micro Calibration

- What trades were taken?
- Were they aligned with the system?
- Any emotional deviations?
- What's the one thing I did well today?
- What's one thing I must improve tomorrow?

Weekly Review: Tactical Refinement

- Total number of trades.
- Win rate, average risk-to-reward, expectancy.

- Most common mistake (theme).
- Was I reactive or disciplined overall?
- What must I reinforce next week?

Monthly Review: Strategic Realignment

- Is my edge still valid in current market conditions?
- What setups are yielding the highest-quality trades?
- What psychological patterns are recurring?
- What boundaries must I set - e.g., max trades per day, no news trades, etc.?

The sniper-trader doesn't just review the *result* - he reviews the *reasoning*.

This process instils two vital forces: **Accountability and Adaptability.**
Without review, you stagnate. With it, you *scale your skill*.

Real-Time Adjustment and Psychological Feedback Loops

Mastery is not built in hindsight alone. The sniper must also make **real-time adjustments** - recalibrating windage, elevation, posture - moment by moment, often mid-mission. His edge lies not in stubborn commitment to a pre-set path, but in his ability to *sense drift early* and correct before damage is done.

For the trader, this means one thing: building a **psychological feedback loop** - a system that catches deviations in mental state, execution discipline, and emotional control *as they occur*.

Why Real-Time Awareness Is Crucial

Most trading errors aren't technical - they're *state-based*. The trader knew the rule. But their state was off.

- Entered too early? That's not a strategy issue. It's *impatience*.

- Held too long? That's not risk management - that's *hope*.

- Skipped a valid setup? That's not analysis - that's *fear*.

Real-time feedback helps you detect these in the moment - not hours later, after damage is done.

How to Build Real-Time Awareness

Pre-Trade Check-In

Before any trade, ask:

- Am I calm or agitated?

- Am I trading from logic or emotion?

- Is this setup fully aligned with my criteria - or am I stretching to justify it?

If any answer triggers doubt, *pause*. Breathe. Reassess. The sniper doesn't rush the shot.

Mid-Trade Monitoring

While the trade is live:

- Am I managing risk or watching P&L?

- Is my exit plan still valid?

- Is my breath shallow or steady?

If your breath is tight, your jaw clenched, your eyes flickering between tabs - you're in a reactive state. Time to reset.

End-of-Session Scan

After your session:

- Was today driven by my system or my emotions?

- What was my dominant emotional state?

- Did I trade with conviction or compulsion?

Capture this in a quick self-assessment log - colour-coded, scored, or simply journaled. Over time, these logs become predictive tools. They show you when to push - and when to step away.

Creating "Interrupt Rituals" to Break Emotional Loops

Sometimes awareness isn't enough. You need a **pattern breaker** - a ritual that disrupts a reactive spiral.

- Stand up. Move. Change your posture.

- Take 3 deep breaths, exhaling for twice as long.

- Use a mantra or internal command: *"Pause. Breathe. Realign."*

- Touch your anchor object - a coin, a stone, a card with your rules.

These are not gimmicks. These are tools of control - rituals that ground you when chaos calls.

The marksman does not train for glory. He trains for reliability. He journals not to collect memories, but to refine execution. He debriefs not to obsess over mistakes, but to extract mastery from them. He adjusts in the moment not because he doubts himself, but because he respects the complexity of the task.

This is the essence of trading discipline.

When you train like a marksman, every trade becomes a teacher.

Your journal becomes your second sight.

Your review becomes your recalibration.

Your awareness becomes your protection.

And slowly - day by day, page by page, breath by breath - you become what most never do:

Not just a trader.

But a professional.

SECTION FOUR

Final Word

The Sniper's Creed

A Manifesto for the Disciplined Trader

"One shot. One kill.

One plan. One purpose.

One life. One standard."

— The Sniper's Way

A sniper is not defined by the rifle he carries or the camouflage he wears. He is defined by the mindset behind the trigger. The *creed* he lives by. The code he does not break — not when the pressure mounts, not when the wind shifts, not even when doubt whispers. His entire art is rooted in restraint. In clarity. In the unshakable discipline to wait for the shot that matters — and let the rest pass.

The trader, too, must live by a code. A set of non-negotiables that protect his edge, preserve his capital, and guide his behaviour. Without a creed, he becomes reactive. Directionless. A drifter in volatile waters. But with a creed — internalised, repeated, honoured — he becomes *fortified*. He becomes resilient under fire. Precise under pressure.

This is **The Sniper's Creed** — a manifesto not of technique, but of *trading character*. It is not a list of rules. It is a declaration of identity.

1. I Will Not Chase Noise — I Will Wait for Clarity

The market will tempt me with movement, rumour, opinion. It will whisper urgency and flash false signals. But I will not be baited. I trade only when my parameters are met. My edge is not in speed — it is in selectivity. I wait for structure. I wait for confirmation. I wait because I am trained to.

The sniper doesn't shoot at shadows — he waits for the silhouette to sharpen.

2. I Will Respect Risk Before I Respect Reward

Profit seduces. The thrill of the win intoxicates. But I will not let desire outpace discipline. My first duty is protection — of capital, of mindset, of longevity. I do not bet — I allocate. I do not gamble — I manage. I am here to survive first, to thrive second.

The sniper carries one bullet with a purpose, not a magazine of wishes.

3. I Will Trade My Plan — Not My Mood

I am not here to feel better. I am here to follow my process. My mood will change. My discipline will not. Whether I am in drawdown or in profit, I will execute according to my system — not according to my emotional state.

The sniper does not flinch with feeling — he breathes through it and stays aligned.

4. I Will Honour the Silence Over the Noise

I do not need to speak to validate my skill. I do not need to be seen to be effective. My trades do not require applause. My growth does not need to be broadcast. I keep my process private because it is sacred.

The sniper's shot is heard only once — after the work is already done.

5. I Will Review, Reflect, and Refine Relentlessly

I am not defined by a single trade, but by the feedback I draw from it. I journal not for record-keeping, but for self-honesty. I debrief not to dwell on mistakes, but to turn them into micro-adjustments. Every shot, every session, every setback — I learn from all.

The sniper dissects every mission — even the successful ones.

6. I Will Stay Centred in Chaos

Markets will crash. Spreads will widen. Slippage will happen. Near-misses will taunt me. But I will not chase revenge, I will not spiral into noise. I will regulate my breath. I will reset my state. I will return to process. I will remain the calmest person on the screen.

The sniper trains his nervous system before he trains his scope.

7. I Will Not Trade to Impress — I Will Trade to Progress

There is no glory in trading for the sake of action. There is no nobility in holding onto losing trades to save face. I release the need to be right. I embrace the duty to be effective. I trade not to show the world — I trade to master myself.

The sniper knows: invisible victories are still victories.

8. I Will Let Go When It's Time

I will exit when the system tells me to — not when my ego does. I will accept when a trade is invalidated — without shame, without force. I will walk away from the screen when my discipline fades — and return only when it is restored. I do not cling. I *release*.

The sniper does not chase the same target twice. He relocates, resets, and re-engages.

9. I Will Master Myself First — The Market Comes Second

The market is not my opponent. My impatience is. My fear is. My doubt, my hope, my distraction — these are the true enemies. If I win over them, I win over the market. My edge is internal. My system is only as strong as the state from which I execute it.

The sniper sharpens not just his rifle — but his mind, his breath, his inner stillness.

10. I Will Trade with Integrity — To Myself and My Craft

There are no shortcuts. No "get rich quick" shots. No substitutes for discipline. I honour my craft. I honour my preparation. I do not break rules. I do not compromise my standards. Even if no one is watching — *I am watching*.

The sniper's code is sacred — even in solitude.

You are not just a trader. You are a precision artist. A decision-maker under fire. A student of your own psychology. A disciple of process. A master in the making.

Let the world rush. Let others shout. Let others chase.

You are a sniper.

You wait.

You align.

You execute.

And then... you disappear.

www.ingramcontent.com/pod-product-compliance
Lightning Source LLC
Chambersburg PA
CBHW020600160726
47991CB00002B/809